Delectable

Recipes

A Complete Cookbook of Delicious Dutch
Dish Ideas!

BY

Julia Chiles

OOOOOOOOOOOOOOOOOOOOOOOOOOOOOOOOOOOOOOOO

License Notes

No part of this Book can be reproduced in any form or by any means including print, electronic, scanning or photocopying unless prior permission is granted by the author.

All ideas, suggestions and guidelines mentioned here are written for informative purposes. While the author has taken every possible step to ensure accuracy, all readers are advised to follow information at their own risk. The author cannot be held responsible for personal and/or commercial damages in case of misinterpreting and misunderstanding any part of this Book

OOOOOOOOOOOOOOOOOOOOOOOOOOOOOOOOOOOOOO

Table of Contents

Introduction

Is Dutch cuisine a real thing? Yes!

It's not as publicized as dishes from many other countries, but they actually have many tasty traditional and fusion dishes that you may enjoy a lot.

You can find all kinds of food in the Netherlands, not just dishes that originated in the country. This cookbook brings you mainly traditional dishes that will give you a true taste of Dutch cuisine. Since some recipes are an integral part of the way of life in the country, trying these dishes helps you to gain a wider experience of their culinary skills.

Since the Netherlands boasts a great deal of international trading and travel, their cuisine has been influenced by other countries. Many dishes are inspired from those found in other countries.

Most of the popular, traditional Dutch dishes are hot, sturdy and filling, to keep you warm and full during the cold winter months. The favored ingredients include those grown in local regions of the Netherlands, like root vegetables, and foods that are pickled, smoked or dried, preserving them to eat on those bitter winter days.

Dutch agriculture brings many ingredients to recipes of the Netherlands. Legumes and grains have been used for many years, and potatoes started as a staple food in the 1700s. Dairy foods are quite beloved, but you'll find lots of other tasty ingredients, too. Turn the page, let's cook!

Dutch Breakfast Recipes

Sweet or savory, Dutch breakfast recipes are tasty and worth getting up for. Here are some of the most popular…

1 – Dutch Mini-Pancakes

These are a special version of miniature Dutch pancakes. Traditionally, they are cooked in unique cast iron pans, and they are based on buckwheat flour, a local staple.

Makes 4 Servings

Cooking + Prep Time: 25 minutes

Ingredients:

- 1 tsp. of yeast, instant
- 1 tbsp. of milk, whole
- 1 cup of flour, buckwheat
- 1 cup of flour, white
- 2 eggs, large
- 1 tsp. of sugar, granulated
- 1/2 tsp. of salt, kosher
- 1 1/4 cups of milk, whole, warm
- 1 tbsp. of butter + extra for serving
- Optional to serve:
- Sugar, confectioner's
- Strawberries
- Whipped cream

Instructions:

1. Dissolve yeast in 1 tbsp. of milk in small sized bowl.

2. In another bowl, combine 1/2 of warm milk, salt, sugar, eggs, flour and milk/yeast mixture. Whisk till you have a smooth texture.

3. Add remainder of warm milk. Beat mixture again.

4. Cover bowl with cling wrap. Allow to rest for one hour.

5. Melt 1 tbsp. of butter in frying pan.

6. When butter begins sizzling, add tsp's. full of batter with circular movements, creating mini pancakes.

7. Turn mini pancakes over when bottoms set.

8. Serve pancakes with high-quality butter. Add confectioner's sugar. They can also be served with powdered sugar, strawberries and whipped cream.

2 – Dutch Breakfast Puffs

If you want something that's easy to make for your breakfast, try Dutch puffs. They are so simple and actually even a little fun to make!

Makes 3-4 Servings

Cooking + Prep Time: 90 minutes + 8 hours sitting time

Ingredients:

- 8 eggs, large
- 2 cups of flour, all-purpose
- 2 cups of milk, whole
- 1/2 tsp. of salt, kosher
- 1 scraped vanilla bean
- 1/2 tsp. of cinnamon, ground
- 5 tbsp. of butter, unsalted

Instructions:

1. Crack the eight eggs into medium bowl. Whisk together well. Then stir in flour, cinnamon, vanilla bean seeds, salt and milk. Expect mixture to be a bit lumpy.

2. Cover bowl with cling wrap. Allow to sit on countertop for the overnight or eight hours.

3. The next day, place the butter in bottom of 13x9" pan. Place pan in oven and heat to 350F.

4. When butter melts, remove from oven. Swirl it around, coating sides and bottom of pan.

5. Remove the cling wrap from egg mixture. Whisk aggressively till no lumps remain. Pour mixture into pan.

6. Bake for 1/2 hour to 45 minutes. Puff should have risen very high. Sides rise quicker, but puff is not done till middle also rises and turns a golden brown in color.

7. Serve with fruit preserves, syrup or powdered sugar.

3 – Dutch Ham Fried Egg Breakfast

This recipe has many variations, but this is the one most commonly cooked. It's made with ham, eggs, cheese and white bread, and it's quick and easy to prepare.

Makes 1 Serving

Cooking + Prep Time: 7-10 minutes

Ingredients:

- 1 tsp. of butter, unsalted
- 2 eggs, large
- 2 white bread slices
- 2 boiled, shaved ham slices
- 2 large cheese slices
- Salt, kosher, as desired
- Pepper, ground, as desired

Instructions:

1. Melt butter in skillet. Fry eggs.

2. Once bottoms of eggs have set, remove pan from heat. Cover. Allow eggs to steam till their tops firm up.

3. Toast bread lightly. Place on plate.

4. Top with ham, cheese and fried eggs.

5. Season as desired. Serve.

4 – Dutch Cinnamon-Vanilla Breakfast Cake

This recipe is called "Ontbijtkoek", which means "breakfast cake" – not a big surprise there. It's like gingerbread but not like American gingerbread. Ontbijtkoek is spicier and chewier. You'll love it!

Makes 8-9 Servings

Cooking + Prep Time: 1 hour + 50 minutes

Ingredients:

- 1 cup of flour, rye
- 1 cup of flour, all-purpose
- 1/2 cup of sugar, brown
- 2 tsp. of baking powder
- 1 1/2 tsp. of ginger, ground
- 1 tsp. of cinnamon, ground
- 1 tsp. of cardamom, ground
- 1/2 tsp. of coriander, ground
- 1/2 tsp. of cloves, ground
- 1/4 tsp. of pepper, black, ground
- 1/4 tsp. of salt, kosher
- 1 cup of milk, whole
- 1/2 cup of honey, organic
- 1/4 cup of molasses
- 1 tsp. of vanilla extract, pure

Instructions:

1. Preheat the oven to 300F. Grease, then flour standard sized loaf pan.

2. Combine all dry ingredients in medium sized bowl.

3. Combine wet ingredients in separate bowl.

4. Pour the wet ingredients into bowl of dry ingredients and stir till you have a smooth consistency. Pour the batter into loaf pan prepared in step 1.

5. Bake for 1 hour 10 minutes to 1 hour 15 minutes. Toothpick inserted in middle of the cake should come back clean.

6. Allow to cool in the pan for 8-10 minutes. Turn cake out on cooling rack till fully cooled.

7. Serve with unsalted butter.

5 – Dutch Apple Bacon Pancakes

In a country with a true love for pancakes, these are probably more famous than the rest. They are hearty and fill a plate, and the combination of flavors is hard to beat.

Makes 8-10 Servings

Cooking + Prep Time: 25 minutes

Ingredients:

- 1 cup of flour, all-purpose
- 1/4 tsp. of baking powder
- 1/2 tsp. of salt, kosher
- 1 cup of milk, whole
- 1 egg, large
- 1 tsp. of butter, unsalted
- 1 tsp. of oil, olive
- 10 bacon rashers, sliced thinly
- 3 peeled, then cored and sliced apples, crisp (like Granny Smith)
- Syrup, your favorite

Instructions:

1. Mix flour, a bit of milk, baking powder and salt to smooth-textured paste. Whisk while you add the rest of the milk slowly.

2. Add egg and beat mixture well.

3. Melt oil and butter in large fry pan. Wait till it is sizzling. Pour in sufficient mixture and cover entire pan surface evenly.

4. Fry till you see bubbles appearing on surface. Turn pancakes over. They should be a pale gold color on each side. Set them aside.

5. Fry bacon in pan till crisp. Remove and allow to drain on paper towels.

6. Add sliced apples to bacon fat. Caramelize them. Drain on plate lined with paper towels.

7. Serve pancakes with bacon and apples and syrup over top.

Dutch Lunch, Dinner, Side Dishes and Appetizers

Here are some delightful Dutch recipes for lunch, dinner, side dishes and appetizers…

6 – Dutch Bacon Meat Rolls - Slavinken

Outside of the Netherlands, this dish is sometimes made with soy sauce and brown sugar, since the traditional sauce used is not commonly made outside the country. The sugar deepens the flavor.

Makes 6 Servings

Cooking + Prep Time: 40 minutes

Ingredients:

- 1/2 pound of beef, ground
- 1/2 pound of pork, ground
- 1 yolk from large egg
- 1/2 cup of bread crumbs
- 1 tsp. of mustard
- 1 1/2 tsp. of Worcestershire sauce
- 1 tsp. of soy sauce, low sodium
- Nutmeg, grated
- Pepper, grated
- 6 thin slices of streaky bacon, rindless
- To fry: 1 tbsp. of butter, unsalted

Instructions:

1. Mix all the ingredients - except for bacon - together.

2. Stretch bacon slices with blunt side of knife.

3. Form meat mixture into six sausage shapes. Wrap bacon slices around them.

4. Melt butter in fry pan over high heat till brown. Then brown the meat rolls on all sides.

5. Reduce heat. Add about 1/2 cup water. Allow to simmer for 12-15 minutes till meat rolls are done and serve.

7 – Cooked Plantains

Baka Bana, or cooked plantains, are easy to make. The recipe has just a few ingredients in addition to the plantains, and it's SO tasty.

Makes 4 Servings

Cooking + Prep Time: 20 minutes

Ingredients:

- 1/2 cup of flour, all-purpose
- 1/2 tsp. of baking soda
- 1 pinch of salt, kosher
- 1/2 cup of water, warm
- 1 ripe, large, sliced plantain
- To fry: vegetable oil

Instructions:

1. Combine the salt, baking soda and flour in medium bowl. Add the warm water and stir constantly till you have a batter like pancake batter.

2. Dip the slices of plantain into batter.

3. Heat oil in deep skillet on med. heat. Cook the plantains in batches till they are golden in color. Flip. Cook for another minute. Drain on the plate lined with paper towels and serve.

8 – Dutch Meatball Tomato Soup

This version of Dutch tomato soup is a bit different from the traditional type. It includes more spices and herbs but is still true to the inspiration of Dutch cooks. The use of turkey for the meatballs **Makes** them healthier.

Makes 4 Servings

Cooking + Prep Time: 2 hours 10 minutes

Ingredients:

For the meatballs

- 8 ounces of turkey, ground
- 2 chopped cloves of garlic
- 1 chopped medium onion
- 2 large eggs, beaten
- 1/4 cup of bread crumbs
- 1/2 tsp. of salt, kosher
- 1/4 tsp. of pepper, ground
- 1 dash nutmeg

For the soup

- 2 tbsp. of oil, olive
- 1 chopped onion, large
- 1 cup of carrots, chopped
- 1 cup of celery, chopped
- 3 chopped cloves of garlic
- 2 bay leaves
- 2 x 28-ounce cans of tomatoes, crushed
- 2 cubes of bouillon
- 1 tsp. of thyme, dried
- 1 tsp. of oregano, dried

- 1 tsp. of paprika
- Kosher salt, as desired
- Ground pepper, as desired

Instructions:

1. Combine meatball ingredients. Mix thoroughly. Form them into meatballs the size of apricots. Chill in fridge for an hour or longer.

2. Heat the oil in large sized pot. Add garlic, celery, carrots and onion. Sauté till the vegetables have softened.

3. Add 4 cups of water, bouillon cubes, crushed tomatoes and bay leaves. Combine well.

4. Add paprika, thyme and oregano and stir, combining well.

5. Bring ingredients to boil. Then reduce to simmer. Cook for 18-20 minutes over low heat.

6. Next, add the meatballs. Simmer for 12-15 minutes, till they have cooked through.

7. Season as desired and serve.

9 - Endive Casserole

If you like dishes with meat and potatoes, you'll love this endive casserole. It is rich-tasting and creamy, and flavored with peppercorns and cheese.

Makes 2 Servings

Cooking + Prep Time: 1 3/4 hour

Ingredients:

- 1 1/2 tbsp. of margarine, reduced calorie
- 1 1/2 tbsp. of flour, all-purpose
- 3/4 cup of milk, skim
- 1/4 tsp. of salt, kosher
- Cooking spray, butter flavored
- 1 1/4 cups of Belgian endive, sliced
- 1 cup of potatoes, peeled and sliced
- 1 1/2 tbsp. of shallot, chopped
- 1/2 oz. of Swiss cheese shreds, reduced fat

Instructions:

1. Melt the margarine in small sauce pan on med. heat. Add flour. Stir till you have a smooth texture.

2. Use wire whisk to stir constantly while cooking for a minute. Add the milk gradually and stir constantly till the white sauce is bubbly and thickened. Remove from the heat and stir in the salt. Set the pan aside.

3. Coat 5 1/4" x 7" x 1 1/2" casserole dish with the cooking spray.

4. Place 1/2 of sliced endives in bottom. Place 1/2 of sliced potatoes on top of the endives. Sprinkle with 1/2 of shallot + 1 tbsp. of cheese. Top using 1/2 of the white sauce.

5. Repeat the layers and end up with white sauce and last 1 tbsp. of cheese on top.

6. Leave uncovered and bake for 40-45 minutes in 350F oven, till potatoes are tender. Serve.

10 – Dutch Fried Fish

Also called "Kibbeling", this dish is often served in the streets of the Netherlands. It's easy to make, too – with pieces of fish dunked in a batter and deep fried. Pair them up with a tasty dipping sauce and they're hard to beat as a snack or appetizer.

Makes 4 Servings

Cooking + Prep Time: 35 minutes

Ingredients:

- 1 1/3 lbs. of chunked fish (white fish works well)
- 5 1/4 oz. of flour, all-purpose
- 6 3/4 fluid oz. of milk, skim
- 1 3/4 fluid oz. of beer or water
- 2 eggs, large
- 1 tsp. of salt, kosher
- 1 tsp. of pepper, ground
- For deep frying: oil
- Spice mix, fish
- Sauce, your favorite type

Instructions:

1. Mix milk with flour, beer (or water), eggs, kosher salt and ground pepper.

2. Preheat deep fryer to 335F.

3. Add fish to batter. Gently stir it around.

4. Slide fish pieces carefully into hot oil one at a time. Do not overcrowd your pan or the oil temperature will drop too much, and the batter will be soggy, not crisp like you want it.

5. When fish pieces are golden brown in color, scoop out with slotted spoon. Place in bowl with paper towels to absorb excess fat and oil.

6. Bake remainder of fish in same manner. Scoop small batter bits out of oil when you change batches.

7. Transfer fish to serving bowl. Sprinkle with the fish spice. Serve hot with your choice of dipping sauces.

11 – Sour Beef Stew

This dish was originally prepared with (gasp) horse meat. I use beef. I also updated the recipe to use my slow cooker, which just **Makes** everything easier.

Makes 4 Servings

Cooking + Prep Time: 40 minutes + 10 hours of "low" slow cooking time

Ingredients:

- 2 1/2 lbs. of beef
- 17 fluid oz. of vinegar, white
- 1 cup of filtered water
- 3 onions, medium
- 1 lb. of apple butter
- 4 slices gingerbread, Dutch
- Salt, kosher, as desired
- Pepper, ground, as desired
- 8 to 10 cloves
- 3 bay leaves

Instructions:

1. Slice the beef in large chunks on cutting board with chef's knife. Set them aside.

2. Quarter your three onions.

3. Place cloves and bay leaves in tea infuser.

4. Heat a deep skillet. Brown beef in oil or butter. Transfer to slow cooker. Use leftover juice to quick-fry onion quarters, then transfer them into slow cooker after a couple minutes.

5. Squeeze in vinegar and sufficient water to submerge meat. Add apple butter. Set slow cooker on LOW for 10 hours.

6. After that 10 hours, meat will be well-cooked and tender. Transfer it into deep skillet, not yet putting in the tea infuser.

7. Raise heat to med-high. Add 3 or 4 slices of gingerbread. Gently stir. Season as desired.

8. Bring to simmer. Wait for most moisture to evaporate. Serve with salad or fries.

12 – Dutch Meatballs

Dutch meatballs are called "Bitterballen" and are served at most any bar in the country. It's a favorite snack with its beef gravy meatballs, and usually it's served with beer.

Makes 4 Servings

Cooking + Prep Time: 1 1/2 hour

Ingredients:

- 1 lb. of pork, veal beef meatloaf mixture, ground
- 4 white bread slices
- 1/3 cup of milk, skim
- 1 beaten egg, large
- 1 finely chopped onion, small
- 1 tbsp. of nutmeg, grated
- 1/2 tsp. of cloves, ground
- Salt, kosher, as desired
- Pepper, black, ground, as desired
- 1/2 cup of butter, unsalted
- 2 cups of water, filtered
- 1 x 14 1/2 oz. can of tomatoes, diced
- 1 x 14-oz. can of broth, beef
- 1 x 1-oz. pkg. of onion soup mix, dry

Instructions:

1. Place the meatloaf mixture in large sized mixing bowl. Crumble the bread over it. Knead by hand and combine well.

2. Add egg and milk to the mixture. Knead in cloves, nutmeg, onions, kosher salt and ground pepper till combined well. Form the mixture into six balls of about the same size.

3. Melt the butter in large pan on med-high. Stir and cook the meatballs in the hot butter till they are brown on each side.

4. Stir the water, onion soup mix and beef broth into same pan. Bring to boil and then reduce the heat down to med-low. Simmer till meatballs are cooked through and tender, or about an hour. Serve.

13 – White Asparagus Soup

This is an innovative way to use tasty white asparagus in a soup all its own. It's made with broth, cream and pureed white asparagus. It has a deep, special flavor.

Makes 6 Servings

Cooking + Prep Time: 1 hour 10 minutes

Ingredients:

- 1/2 cup of chopped onion
- 2 tbsp. of butter, unsalted
- 1 1/2 – 2 lbs. of asparagus, white, peeled, sliced in 2" pieces with reserved heads
- 6 cups of veggie or chicken broth
- 1/2 cup of half n half
- Salt, as desired
- Pepper, ground, as desired
- White wine, dry, as desired
- For garnishing: parsley

Instructions:

1. Sauté onion in butter in bottom of 4-qt. sauce pan till soft.

2. Add asparagus pieces except heads. Steam for three to five minutes.

3. Add broth. Gently boil for 1/2 hour. Asparagus should be quite soft.

4. Puree soup in small batches in blender.

5. Bring soup to simmer. Add heads of asparagus.

6. Cook for five minutes or a bit longer, till heads of asparagus become tender.

7. Reduce heat. Add half n half. Don't allow mixture to boil.

8. Season as desired. Use parsley to garnish and serve.

14 – Poached Pears in Red Wine

This is an easy but delectable recipe for pears poached in wine. There are very few ingredients, and you can serve the pears cold or warm.

Makes 4 Servings

Cooking + Prep Time: 2 hours 50 minutes

Ingredients:

- 4 peeled, then cored quartered large pears, firm
- 1 stick of cinnamon
- 1/2 cup of sugar, granulated
- 1 orange peel
- 5 glasses of wine, red

Instructions:

1. Place the pears in sauce pan. Add cinnamon stick, sugar and orange peel. Add red wine sufficient to completely cover the pears.

2. Bring to boil, then reduce the heat and gently simmer till pears become a deep red color and are soft. This usually takes about 2 1/2 hours.

3. Transfer the pears to serving plate. Serve warm or allow to cool and serve.

15 – Sausage Rolls

These sausage rolls make a wonderful snack, and a great carry-in for a potluck or party. If you have any leftovers (don't count on it) they store well in the fridge.

Makes 32 Sausage rolls

Cooking + Prep Time: 40 minutes

Ingredients:

- 1 pound of ground beef, lean
- 1 egg, large
- 2 tbsp. of milk, skim
- 1 tsp. of salt, kosher
- 1/8 tsp. nutmeg, ground
- Pepper, ground, as desired
- 1/2 cup of breadcrumbs, panko
- 1 tsp. of Worcestershire sauce
- 4 thawed sheets of puff pastry
- 1 yolk from large egg
- 1 tsp. of water, filtered

Instructions:

1. Preheat the oven to 400F. Line cookie sheet with baking paper. Set it aside.

2. Unfold the sheets of puff pastry. Cut each sheet in half lengthways, creating eight separate sheets.

3. In large sized bowl, use your hands to gently but quickly combine the first eight ingredients above. Divide into eight portions of equal size.

4. Roll each portion into sausage shape. Place in middle of sheet of puff pastry, across length of sheets.

5. Fold pastry sheets around sausage shaped meat pieces. Wet your fingers and pinch top, then bottom edges to bring them together and enclose "sausage". Cut each one into four pieces of equal size, forming 32 sausage rolls total.

6. Beat the egg yolk with 1 tsp. of water. Brush this over rolls.

7. Place sausage rolls on cookie sheet and place sheet in middle of 400F oven. Bake for 18-20 minutes. Pastry should be golden and crisp. Serve while warm.

16 – Split Pea Soup

The name for this soup is "snert", which is an odd name, to be sure. This is a modern take on "snert" and uses a slow cooker. You still need to babysit it, since it requires stirring and having water added if needed.

Makes 8 Servings

Cooking + Prep Time: 35 minutes + 7 hours slow cooker time

Ingredients:

- 1 x 14-oz. bag of split peas, dried
- 3 chopped bacon slices
- 1 ham hock
- 2 x 14 1/2 oz. cans of broth, chicken
- 3 1/2 cups of water, filtered, + extra if needed
- 2 peeled, diced carrots
- 4 small peeled, diced potatoes
- 1 diced leak
- 1/2 large diced onion
- 2 celery stalks – with diced stalks and chopped leaves
- 1 diced garlic clove
- 1/2 tsp. of salt, kosher
- 1/2 tsp. of pepper, black, ground
- 1/2 tsp. of thyme, dried
- 1/2 tsp. of nutmeg, ground
- 1/4 tsp. of cloves, ground
- 1 lb. of sliced sausage, smoked

Instructions:

1. Place the ham hock, bacon and split peas in slow cooker. Add broth and water.

2. Cover the slow cooker. Cook on the high setting till peas become tender and have broken apart. This usually takes three to four hours. Add more water if you need it, so the soup won't burn on bottom. Stir occasionally while cooking.

3. Stir while adding garlic, celery, onions, leek, carrots and potatoes to soup. Mix in additional water if you need it. Cover. Cook the soup on the high setting for two additional hours.

4. Season as desired. Mix the sliced sausage into the soup. Cover. Cook for two hours longer, so the flavors can blend fully. Serve.

17 - Dutch Salmon Pie

It's always nice to have go-to recipes that are easy to make even on weekday, workday evenings. You can add corn and pineapple if you like, but this is a simpler version.

Makes 8 Servings

Cooking + Prep Time: 35 minutes

Ingredients:

- 1 x 14 3/4 oz. can of salmon, red or pink
- 1 pkg. of cheese, Boursin, with herbs and garlic
- 1 shallot, small
- 1 tbsp. of breadcrumbs

- 3 tbsp. of diced green and red peppers
- 3 eggs, large
- 1 sheet of puff pastry
- 1 bunch of parsley, fresh

Instructions:

1. Drain salmon. Break meat into large pieces and pick out bones and skin.

2. Beat the eggs with 1/2 of cheese. Chop shallot. Fold it into eggs.

3. Rolled thawed pastry in 9" pie form and poke holes using a fork. Cover with 1 tbsp. of panko or breadcrumbs.

4. Distribute salmon chunks evenly on bottom of pie form. Pour the eggs over the salmon. Spread remainder of cheese over eggs. Sprinkle bell pepper atop the mixture.

5. Heat oven to 400 degrees F. Bake salmon pie for 20 minutes till it is done. The egg should be solid by then. You can finish the pie under broiler if you like. It will add color.

6. Sprinkle with parsley and serve.

18 – Dutch Mustard Soup

In the Netherlands, this dish is made with zaanse mustard, which is coarse and has seeds. Once you have warm soup, serve it up with fresh baked bread for a wonderful treat.

Makes 8 Servings

Cooking + Prep Time: 40 minutes

Ingredients:

- 1 pound of diced bacon
- 3 tbsp. of butter, unsalted
- 1/3 cup of flour, all-purpose
- 1 qt. of stock, chicken
- 2 yolks from large eggs
- 1 cup of cream, heavy
- 1/2 cup of mustard, coarse grain
- 1 peeled, then cored diced apple, Granny Smith

Instructions:

1. Cook bacon while stirring occasionally in large skillet on med. heat till it is evenly browned and crisp.

2. Pour the fat away. Drain bacon on plate lined with paper towels.

3. Melt butter in sauce pan on med-low. Add flour. Stir till mixture is golden brown and paste-like.

4. Whisk chicken stock gradually into flour mixture. Bring to simmer on med. heat. Stir and cook till mixture becomes smooth and thick. Reduce the heat down to low.

5. Beat heavy cream and egg yolks together till blended well. Whisk 1/4 of hot soup slowly into cream mixture. Return new cream mixture to pot. Whisk in mustard and stir in bacon and apple. Stir while cooking till soup becomes hot, but not yet simmering. Serve.

19 – Endive Stew

Ah, this is "Stamppot", a wonderful, old-fashioned Dutch dish. It's basically mashed potatoes with one or two other vegetables included.

Makes 6-8 Servings

Cooking + Prep Time: 55 minutes

Ingredients:

- 1 1/3 pound of potatoes
- 14 ounces of endive, escarole
- 1 tsp. of salt, kosher
- 6 slices of bacon

Instructions:

1. Peel potatoes. Cut in medium chunks. Bring them to boil in pot with water barely covering potatoes. Add salt. Reduce heat down to med. Boil for 20 minutes.

2. Fry bacon in skillet. When done, cut in small strips.

3. When you can pierce the potatoes easily with a fork, pour off rest of water. Save 1/2 cup. Mash the potatoes. Add some of the potato water if they get dry while mashing.

4. Wash escarole and rinse. Cut in 1/2" strips. Mix with potatoes. Add bacon. Season as desired and serve.

20 – Witlof Ham

"Witlof", or endive, is used in this wonderful appetizer. It came to the region by way of Belgium, but it's quite popular in the Netherlands, too.

Makes 4 Servings

Cooking + Prep Time: 30 minutes

Ingredients:

- 4 heads of endive, medium
- 4 x 1/2-oz. slices of prosciutto
- 1 cup of Gruyere cheese, grated

Instructions:

1. Prepare grill for med. heat. As soon as it's ready, brush lightly using oil.

2. Place endive in shallow casserole dish. Add 1/4 cup water. Cover using cling wrap. Microwave for a couple minutes, till just a bit tender. Remove from the dish. Pat endive dry.

3. Wrap whole endive with prosciutto. Secure with toothpicks. Place pieces directly on the grill. Turn occasionally while cooking till endive is tender and ham has browned.

4. Place in foil baking dish. Sprinkle with cheese. Return to grill and cover. Cook till cheese melts. Serve.

21 – Rib Roast Carrots

"Hutspot" includes braised beef and carrots, and if you can find winter carrots like Autumn King or Flakkee, they work best. If not, then regular carrots will work fine. The flavor just won't be as robust.

Makes 4-6 Servings

Cooking + Prep Time: 3 1/4 hours

Ingredients:

- 1 pound of rib roast, beef chuck
- 13 1/2 fluid ounces of water, filtered
- 1/2 cube of beef bouillon
- 1 bay leaf
- 8 whole peppercorns, black
- 1 tbsp. of flour – dissolve in a half-cup of water
- 6 peeled, quartered large potatoes
- 8 peeled, diced large carrots
- 4 peeled, sliced large onions
- Salt, kosher, and pepper, ground

Instructions:

1. Add water to large pan. Add bouillon cube. Stir till it dissolves.

2. Add beef, peppercorns and bay leaf. Braise over low heat for about 90 minutes. Beef should be tender.

3. Remove meat to serving dish. Discard peppercorns and bay leaf. Stir dissolved flour into juices from pan. Scrape bottom of pan and loosen particles of meat that might have stuck there.

4. Bring heat up gradually till gravy begins thickening. Pour gravy over meat. Set it aside and keep it warm.

5. Place potatoes on bottom of pan. Add water till potatoes are barely covered. Add the carrots and onions and salt as desired.

6. Cover. Bring mixture to boil. Lower heat. Boil for 15-20 minutes, till potatoes have cooked fully. Pour off cooking water and reserve it.

7. Mash potatoes, onions and carrots till the mixture has the consistency of mashed potatoes. You can add a bit of cooking liquid if you need to. Taste and adjust seasonings as desired.

8. Serve on large platter, family style, with sliced beef and gravy.

22 – Gouda Cheese Dip

The Dutch love their cheese, and Gouda is one of their favorites. Even if you don't really LIKE Gouda, you will probably surprise yourself and still enjoy this dish, served with pita chips, baguette slices or crackers.

Makes 12 Servings

Cooking + Prep Time: 1/2 hour

Ingredients:

- 2 1/8 cups of mayonnaise, reduced fat
- 2 cups of Gouda cheese, smoked and shredded
- 1 cup of Gouda cheese w/chipotle peppers, shredded
- 3/4 cup of onion, chopped
- 4 oz. of chopped bacon, cooked

Instructions:

1. Preheat the oven to 350F.

2. Mix the mayo, Gouda and the Gouda with peppers, along with bacon and onion together in medium bowl. Spread into casserole dish.

3. Bake in 350F oven till mixture is lightly browned around edges and bubbly. This usually takes 15-20 minutes. Serve.

23 – Dutch Kale Sausage

If it's chilly out, many Dutch cooks will be making this cold-weather food. The hearty taste of kale and Brussels sprouts is perfect for those cold winter days.

Makes 7-9 Servings

Cooking + Prep Time: 1 1/4 hour

Ingredients:

- 1 pound of kale, fresh
- 2 1/4 pounds of potatoes
- 9 ounces of butter, unsalted
- 1 3/4 ounces of warm milk, whole
- 1 x 9- 3/4-ounce sausage, smoked
- 1 pinch salt, kosher

Instructions:

1. Wash kale. Rip leaves from stems, slicing them into thin strips.

2. Peel potatoes, then quarter and put in large pot. Add just enough water to cover potatoes. Add kale, then smoked sausage.

3. Cover pot. Bring to boil. Boil over low flame for 15-20 minutes, till potatoes have cooked.

4. Remove sausage. Pour off cooking liquid remaining. Mash veggies.

5. Add milk and butter. Stir into your puree. Taste and season as desired.

6. Slice sausage and add to veggies. Add mustard as desired. Serve.

24 – Leek Casserole

Leek casserole is a full meal on its own and another cold weather favorite. It's usually eaten as soon as it comes out of the oven.

Makes 8 Servings

Cooking + Prep Time: 1 1/4 hour

Ingredients:

- 2 lbs. of peeled, chopped potatoes
- 1/4 cup of milk, 2%
- 2 lbs. of chopped leeks
- 1 lb. of beef, ground
- 1 chopped onion
- 2 chopped bell peppers, 1 red 1 green
- 1 tbsp. green chilies, chopped finely
- Soy sauce, as desired
- 8 oz. of cheddar cheese shreds
- 6 oz. of thinly sliced ham, cooked

Instructions:

1. Preheat the oven to 350F.

2. Bring large sized pot of lightly salted water to boil. Cook potatoes for 12-15 minutes till firm but tender. Drain the potatoes. Transfer them to medium sized bowl. Mash them together with the milk.

3. Place the leeks in sauce pan with water sufficient to cover them. Bring to boil and cook for 10 minutes, till leeks are tender. Drain. Set aside.

4. In skillet on med. heat, stir while cooking ground beef till it has browned evenly. Add bell peppers and onions. Season using green chilies with soy sauce. Then continue cooking and stirring till veggies have become tender.

5. In medium sized casserole dish, mix potatoes, ground beef and leeks and veggies. Sprinkle using cheddar cheese. Add ham on top.

6. Bake for 22-28 minutes at 350F till lightly browned and bubbly. Serve.

25 – Dutch Meat Vegetable Soup

This recipe uses 1/2 beef and 1/2 pork to create its signature taste. The fat in the pork ensures that your meatballs will be tender and juicy.

Makes 2-3 Servings

Cooking + Prep Time: 1 hour 10 minutes

Ingredients:

- 5 1/3 ounces of pork, ground
- 5 1/3 ounces of beef, ground
- 1 tbsp. of bread crumbs
- 1/4 tsp. of nutmeg, ground
- 1/2 tsp. of salt, kosher
- 1/2 tsp. of pepper, ground
- 34 fluid ounces of bouillon in water
- 7 ounces of vegetables for soup

Instructions:

1. Mix meats with bread crumbs, nutmeg, kosher salt ground pepper till blended well. Roll the mixture into small sized meatballs – about marble-sized.

2. Heat bouillon to slow boil. Then add fresh veggies. Simmer for 20-25 minutes.

3. Place a few meatballs at once in bouillon. Wait for 10 seconds. Add more, several at a time, till all meatballs are in soup. These meatballs are called "soepballetjes" in the Netherlands.

4. When meatballs float, within one or two minutes, they are done. Serve soup with meatballs when all have cooked.

Dutch Dessert Recipes

Dutch desserts are SO good! You'll want to try some of these recipes…

26 – Apple Beignets

This treat is often described as a hybrid of doughnuts and apple pies. It's made quite a lot in the winter time, for a cold weather dessert.

Makes 12 Servings

Cooking + Prep Time: 35 minutes

Ingredients:

- 1 tsp. + 1/4 cup of sugar, granulated
- 1/2 cup of filtered water, lukewarm
- 4 1/2 tsp. of dry yeast, instant
- 4 cups of flour, all-purpose
- 2 eggs, large
- 2 cups of milk, whole
- 1 tsp. of salt, kosher
- To fry: 8 cups of oil, vegetable
- 6 apples, medium sized
- For garnishing: ground cinnamon and powdered sugar

Instructions:

1. In small sized bowl, mix a tsp. of granulated sugar in 1/2 cup lukewarm water. Sprinkle yeast over top. Allow to stand for about 10 minutes. The yeast should bubble. Combine by stirring and set the bowl aside.

2. Mix 1/4 cup of sugar and flour in large sized bowl. Make indentation in center. Add eggs and yeast mixture.

3. Warm milk in microwave till lukewarm. Add 1/2 of it to indentation. Mix till all the ingredients have combined well. Add remainder of milk. Whisk till you have a smooth texture.

4. Cover bowl with damp, clean dish towel. Allow it to sit in warm area to rise for an hour or so. After dough is doubled in size, add salt and stir. Dough should be quite slack and be almost like a thick batter.

5. Heat oil in deep pan to 350F. Peel, then core and slice apples into rounds that are fairly thick. Use tweezers or fingers to dip apple slices into dough. Shake off excess batter, if any. Drop each apple round gently into heated oil.

6. Fritters will first sink to bottom and then they will pop back up. Fry about six or seven at a time, till golden on both sides. Flip once to make sure both sides are done. Drain on paper towel-lined plate.

7. Sieve the powdered sugar over apple beignets and dust with cinnamon. Serve while still warm.

27 - Dutch Pastry Log

Known as "Banket", this Dutch dish is especially popular during the Christmas holidays. It features puff pastry stuffed with orange zest and almond paste. It's amazingly good.

Makes 10 Servings

Cooking + Prep Time: 40 minutes

Ingredients:

- 14-ounce sheet of frozen/thawed puff pastry
- 10 ounces of almond paste
- 1 zested orange
- 1 beaten egg, large
- 3 tbsp. of jam, apricot
- 1 tbsp. of sugar, powdered
- 2 tbsp. of almonds, sliced
- 3 tbsp. of flour, all-purpose

Instructions:

1. Preheat oven to 425F. Cover cookie sheet with baking paper.

2. Flour your work surface lightly. Roll puff pastry out into large-sized rectangle, two inches shorter than cookie sheet. Halve the pastry lengthways.

3. Combine orange zest and almond paste in medium-sized bowl. Knead till blended well.

4. Divide almond mixture into two pieces of the same size. Roll them into logs about an inch shorter than puff pastry length.

5. Place an almond log on 1/2 of the puff pastry. Brush sides of pastry with beaten egg.

6. Fold the two shorter ends of pastry and cover almond log. Fold the two longer ends over almond log. Flip log so seam is at bottom.

7. Repeat with second puff pastry sheet.

8. Transfer logs onto cookie sheet. Brush with beaten egg. Bake for 25 minutes or so till they are browned slightly on the top.

9. Place apricot jam in plastic or glass dish. Heat for 20-30 seconds or so in microwave till jam becomes runny.

10. Brush the baked logs with apricot jam. Then sprinkle them with the almond slices. Dust with powdered sugar. Serve with coffee or tea.

28 – Dutch Fruit Pudding

The Dutch version of fruit pudding uses maraschino liqueur, and its cherry flavor, to round out the tastes. The pudding is made from whipping cream and gelatin.

Makes 10 Servings

Cooking + Prep Time: 45 minutes

Ingredients:

- 1 large egg, free-range
- 4 yolks from large eggs
- 1/2 cup of sugar, granulated
- 5 leaves of gelatin, sheets
- 1/3 cup of water, filtered
- 1 tbsp. of rum
- 5 tsp. of maraschino liqueur
- 2 1/4 cup of whipping cream + extra if desired
- 2 cups of fresh fruit, chopped, any fruit except kiwi or pineapple
- 1/4 cup of amaretto biscuits
- For garnishing: fruit, fresh

Instructions:

1. Whisk together egg yolks, egg and 1/2 sugar in double boiler till they thicken.

2. Soak gelatin sheet in cold, filtered water. Warm it gently in small sized sauce pan on low heat till gelatin dissolves. Add to egg mixture with liqueur and rum. Mix well and allow it to cool.

3. Beat cream with remainder of sugar till it will hold soft peaks. Next, fold cream through cooled egg mixture.

4. Add fruit and amaretti biscuits to mixture. Spoon into dampened pudding mold.

5. Leave pudding to sit in refrigerator for a day, allowing flavors to deepen and mix.

6. To turn pudding out, immerse mold briefly in heated water. Cover with large platter. Slip mold and plate. Remove mold. Decorate your dessert with fruit extra whipped cream, as desired. Serve.

29 – Dutch Butter Cake

For a long time the Dutch have been known for their buttery, rich cake, known as "Boterkoek". It's similar to shortbread, but richer and softer.

Makes 1 pan – various size servings

Cooking + Prep Time: 45 minutes

Ingredients:

- 2 cups of flour, all-purpose
- 8 oz. of butter, unsalted
- 2/3 cup of sugar, granulated
- 1/4 tsp. of salt, kosher

Instructions:

1. Preheat the oven to 350F. Line an 8-inch square baking pan with an aluminum foil.

2. Melt butter. Mix with flour, salt and sugar till barely combined. Do not overmix it. Press it into bottom of baking pan.

3. Bake for 1/2 hour in 350F oven, till edges begin turning golden brown. The middle at this time will still be quite gooey but cake itself is done.

4. Allow the cake to cool fully before you remove foil from the pan and cut cake in squares. Serve.

30 – Brandied, Spiced Raisins

Brandy is a long-used means of preserving wines and fruit in the Netherlands. Brandied fruits are still very popular, and easy to make, too.

Makes 16 Servings

Cooking + Prep Time: 1/2 hour

Ingredients:

- 1 1/4 cups of sugar, brown
- 1 cup of water, filtered
- Zest from 1 lemon
- 3 1/3 cups of raisins, sultana if available
- 1 tsp. of honey, organic
- 1 tsp. of vanilla extract, pure
- 1 stick of cinnamon
- 1 clove
- 1 quart of brandy

Instructions:

1. Add water and sugar to sauce pan. Cook on med. heat till sugar dissolves.

2. Pare off 2 thin strips from lemon's peel. Add to sauce pan. Add spices, vanilla, honey and raisins.

3. Cook over low heat till fruit swells and softens.

4. Bring to boil. Use slotted spoon to scoop raisins into two sterilized jam jars.

5. Reduce remaining liquid till mixture has thickened.

6. Remove from heat. Allow mixture to cool. Remove spices and zest. Pour the liquid over raisins. Add brandy.

7. Tightly seal jars. Shake. Store in dark, cool place for six weeks or longer before serving or eating. After you open the jars, refrigerate them.

Conclusion

This Dutch cookbook has shown you…

How to use different ingredients to affect unique tastes from the Netherlands in dishes both well-known and rare.

How can you include Dutch recipes in your home repertoire?

You can…

- Make delicious Dutch breakfasts that are tasty and will fill you up until it's time for lunch.
- Learn to cook with jams and jellies, which are widely used in the Netherlands. Find them in jam at ethnic or European type food markets.
- Enjoy making poffertjes (baby pancakes) and Bitterballen (savory meatballs), which are quite authentic Dutch dishes.
- Make meals that include split pea soup or Stamppotor (mashed potatoes with other vegetables).

- Make various types of desserts like spiced raisins or butter cake and Dutch treats that will tempt your family's sweet tooth.

Have fun experimenting! Enjoy the results!

Author's Afterthoughts

Thanks ever so much to each of my cherished readers for investing the time to read this book!

I know you could have picked from many other books, but you chose this one. So, a big thanks for reading all the way to the end. If you enjoyed this book or received value from it, I'd like to ask you for a favor. Please take a few minutes to ***post an honest and heartfelt review on*** *Amazon.com.* Your support does make a difference and helps to benefit other people.

Thanks!

Julia Chiles

About the Author

Julia Chiles

(1951-present)

Julia received her culinary degree from Le Counte' School of Culinary Delights in Paris, France. She enjoyed cooking more than any of her former positions. She lived in Montgomery, Alabama most of her life. She married Roger

Chiles and moved with him to Paris as he pursued his career in journalism. During the time she was there, she joined several cooking groups to learn the French cuisine, which inspired her to attend school and become a great chef.

Julia has achieved many awards in the field of food preparation. She has taught at several different culinary schools. She is in high demand on the talk show circulation, sharing her knowledge and recipes. Julia's favorite pastime is learning new ways to cook old dishes.

Julia is now writing cookbooks to add to her long list of achievements. The present one consists of favorite recipes as well as a few culinary delights from other cultures. She expands everyone's expectations on how to achieve wonderful dishes and not spend a lot of money. Julia firmly believes a wonderful dish can be prepare out of common household staples.

If anyone is interested in collecting Julia's cookbooks, check out your local bookstores and online. They are a big seller whatever venue you choose to purchase from.

Printed in Great Britain
by Amazon